A Brief History of the Midwest

A Brief History of the Midwest

Andrew Grace

Black Lawrence Press

Black Lawrence Press

Executive Editor: Diane Goettel
Cover and Interior Design: Zoe Norvell
Cover Artwork: "Animal Psychology" by Leslie Norman

Copyright © Andrew Grace
2025

ISBN: 978-1-62557-1-588

All rights reserved. Except for brief quotations in critical articles or reviews, no part of this book may be reproduced in any manner without prior written permission from the publisher: editors@blacklawrencepress.com

Published 2025 by Black Lawrence Press.
Printed in the United States.

For Tory, For Lily, For Claire

Table of Contents

- 1   I
- 3   A Brief History of the Midwest
- 4   Not a Mile
- 6   The Hive
- 8   For the Silo Boys
- 9   Hell is Real
- 10   Necessity is the Mother
- 12   God's Country
- 13   Agriculture
- 14   What I Know
- 15   Do You Consider Writing to Be Therapeutic?

- 17   II

- 19   Knox County

- 31   III

- 33   Field Guide for How to Pioneer the Midwest
- 39   —black frost plenty: A Primer for Farmwives
- 44   The End of the Midwest

- 49   IV

- 51   Boyne River Daybook

- 77   Notes
- 79   Acknowledgments

*Mine was a Midwest home—
you can keep your world.*

—WILLIAM STAFFORD

I.

A Brief History of the Midwest

History is really the history of thistle.

Thistle: Pliny's cure for baldness.
A thistle destroyed a Norse army
when it pierced the foot of a hidden soldier.
Crest of a kingdom, thistle, the endless.

Thistle cleaves to sheep the color of nicotine.
The farmer knows its language:
Common, Milk, Sow, Star, Blessed.
Prongs of thistles hector the farmer's crotch.

The seams of the Midwest are stitched by thistle

and a field of thistle hoards its seeds in its chest
until thistledown and finch grift its clutch.
Its morning blossoms are pink as raw salt.
They are shorn and gathered into a pile to burn.

Seeds will spread, borne on carbon to new radii.
Thus the next acreage taken by its thorns.
Thistle and ditch become synonymous.
The hills lay down their shadows like Tarot cards.

The history of the Midwest is written in thorn.

Not a Mile

from where my students ask me
why Sylvia Plath wanted to eat men,
two men overdose. This is rural Ohio,
and the new drugs from Columbus
are cut with elephant tranquilizers.
The police are nurses now.
They don't dream. My students try
to understand why the voice
in the poem brags about death, but
never dies. Not a mile from here,
two men regain consciousness
in their living room full of litter boxes
and Optimos. They are not particularly scared
by the police or their IVs. They have both
died before, and been revived with Narcan.
It's November 6th, and the sky
has been blank for so long its emptiness
has turned supple. The men refuse
further medical treatment. One dumps
a baggie of crickets into a lizard tank.
My students are sincerely trying
to analyze death: its cadence and anaphora,
its German origins. The police
do not know how to speak
to my students. They bark and lord
over a scuffle or jaywalking
because they are used to hauling the dead
back to life and fishing names

out of their mouths. They cannot help
but see everyone as needing to be saved
by force. Not a mile from where my students
show me outlines of what they are trying
to say about resurrection, one of the men
pulls a phone out of his mesh shorts
and calls Columbus. My students worry
they cannot explain where Plath ends
and death begins. Not a mile
from our classroom, men dissolve
like powder in water. Men so close
we can't see them. Men like air.

The Hive

In the *Georgics*, Virgil tells me
to empty out my small tool shed
and lure in a young bull,
two years old, stop up
his nostrils with greased rags
and force sand or mud down his throat
until he collapses, then take some
of the hammers I've just thrown into the grass
and pound his flanks until his insides
lose their shape. Virgil tells me to pull
branches down from my dying alder
and cover the bull with them,
as well as sprigs of marjoram and thyme.
It should be done in April.
As light warms the bull's stomach,
deep within white creatures
with blind amber eyes are born
and find their way into the air.
They swarm and unloose their wings
and churn as one into my bee box
making a noise like a machine
with bad alignment, or
ripped subwoofers in the cars
of boys who tattoo tears
on their faces as if we needed proof
of their suffering. Virgil says
to find the queen and rip off her wings
so the flock will never flee.

Plant saffron, pines. He never again
seems to mention the bull, what to do
with its body after giving birth
to drudges of sweetness,
whether to burn the entire shed
in its privacy of rust,
or to wait until there are only bones
to haul out like a galleon's wreckage.
The bull waits, as if in obedience.
My fingers scan *Georgics*, taking its pulse.
The hive stokes its feral sugars.

For the Silo Boys

When the corn gave,
a boy was sucked to the bottom
of the cement silo whose walls
he was paid almost nothing
to scrape clean with a steel pole.
It took 35 men to pull his body
from the outlet spout.

Corn had plugged his nostrils,
ears and throat as far down
as his lungs. In the calf barn,
rescuers cleared the field
of his face, a few fistfuls of grain
a calf sluggishly ate
on its way out to pasture.

In the *Iliad*, the moment
Dolon, young, ugly, volunteered
to spy on the Argives when
no one else would, he was doomed
to have his weasel cap stripped
while his head rolled into a trench
darkened with other sons' blood

where his mouth would slowly fill
with blades of grass.

Hell is Real

There is no
Jesus Jesus enough for Ohio
according to billboards
announcing Ohio as simply Hell,
its river scum made of midge shucks,
its hills of shale.

It's all spray painted:
underpass, boxcar, lamb.
The billboards publish Hell
across leaked snow.

If only Ohio held a graceful detachment
from being Ohio.
If only Ohio's Jesus
would come back,
if only, heaven notwithstanding,
there was an Ohio Ohio enough.

Necessity is the Mother

Instead of a knob on the grain truck's gearshift
                                                  a wad of paper towel.
Instead of a house key a credit card.
                            My mother
kept the books.
               There was always
                           a bird trapped in
the chimney.
                   She and I lifted dead kittens
                                  born in an abandoned boat
fallen into its keel. There was always some killing
                                   to do. Mother
made
     herself into the Picasso of health insurance.
                                       Who else?
Our fields were full of futures and we hauled them in.
                                       Her father
was not the only welder.
                  She cut the tip of her finger
off and held us.
              The house almost burned.
                               I gave away our good sheets
to stop bleeding at a wreck on 45.
                  At church
                           we looked like other families.
No one could tell
             the vastness we tried to explain
                                 ourselves to.

She arranged
> our silences.
>> Filed them alphabetically.
Her husband died.
> Later that day,
>> her father did too.
She balanced the books.
> Remarried.
>> Succeeded the losses.
Invented a life
> yet untitled.
>> What else? she surely
asked the water softener,
> the Hicksgas propane tank.
Nothing else answered
> zeros in her ledger. Each stitch's X.
Nothing else.

God's Country

The scat got fresher
as I
climbed up in our old pig sty.
I scared
a fox
who somehow ran down
without stairs.
I watched it from the window
flee towards
the house where I was a boy.
Now I was alone.
There was no more God there.
No less.
A heart-colored animal
lived there
and now flicks amok
in the far forty.
If it thought I was a God
and this my country
it knew
enough to become in black grass
black grass.

Agriculture

The panicked buck
ran completely underneath the sprayer,

almost clearing the chassis
save both antlers,
ten pointed, which broke off
on the bulkhead.

When dawn came, the antlers
were little skeleton trees
in a new forest,
a dead one

that won't accept death any more
than spring can.

What I Know

It is the hour
when the muscles
of my heart stitch
their crooked quilt of blood.

Horizon swallows houses
like a snake.

A broken engine
is a convict forever confessing
his one kill.

We are only able
to understand one landscape.

Acres of quail.
Fence-lines that wander
like pilgrims.
The simple, unbearable stars.

Do You Consider Writing to Be Therapeutic?

After my father died
I should have gone to therapy.
I tried instead to solve my grief
with alcohol and poems.
Now I am almost 40
and all I can tell you about grief
is that when I found my father
on the floor of the machine shed
the radio was on and wind
pushed against corrugated metal.
Of course I still hear it.
I should have talked
to someone before now
and not you. Poetry is not talking.
This is just art
and therefore could never
cover my ears when I, suddenly,
am back in the shed
and I learn again that my father
has died every day
since he died.

II.

Knox County

Where mill
        collapsed
                into north fork

life floods
        nothing
                can be kept out

We live
        softly
                in a hard place

window factory
        factory
                of oil traps

it gets so dark
        women
                wear whistles

when danger comes
        they call to each other
                like kingfishers

Hope is in movement
        curving
                of water

    back upon itself
        pageant
            of rills

pour into tributary
        one named for a poet
            another for wolf

B&O once coursed
        along bank now a trail
            men jog

tell my daughter
        on her silver bike
            they could do any

thing they want to
        to her
            there's no one

else around
        only horses
            their blue

shadows only herons
        whose rookery
            is where quarry

meets Kokosing
        only railroad worm
            also known

as apple maggot fly
>   spray them with tanglefoot
>   > if needed begin

checking traps every day
>   chemical curl
>   > in eddy

catfish color of
>   unpainted barns
>   > who eat frogs

slow grass
>   gudgeon blue
>   > berry corn

Wind is a flood
>   too it lets itself in
>   > like a late father

like a CPS
>   wellness check
>   > Thunder with no

rain like a false cast
>   what else
>   > but read more

watch Norse pine
>   shiver here
>   > come vultures

  one by one
    soon festooned
      so thick

they go white
  from scat
    of those above them

takeoff
  to find where death
    meets sun

A mother was murdered
  also her friend
    her son

KILLER STUFFED
  HIS HOUSE
    WITH LEAVES

KEPT KIDNAPPED GIRL
  ON BED OF LEAVES
    "He was killing

squirrels because
  he doesn't
    grocery shop"

hid bodies
  in a hollow tree
    lowered them

   in with a pulley
        parked by river
                until caught

made them promise
        not to cut his tree down
                they did

Rolls Royce factory
        closed public
                library open

To read more
        closely is to love
                more closely

Night comes we need it
        biologically
                darkness

to rest or to feed
        trees practice
                for winter

each dusk
        draw deeper
                within themselves

not just bats
        but us we need dark
                to see our

  world not
     remember itself
        then see again

light
    only then
       is it fact

Kingfisher asymptote
    from creek
       to wire

Small's Sand
    & Gravel
       cold pedestal

on which seed
    is placed
       titmice

carry it off
    rookery stocked
       with fledglings

so ungainly
    even those nested
       seem orphan

herons stalk
    neck an S
       over shad

loosed to stab
    then lift
        bright prey

A hard place
    cold oil
        black paste

We live softly
    watch pageants
        of dust

spill from
    combines
        like Doré's

corkscrew of souls
    in *Inferno*
        "fury drives

spirits on"
    crop dust
        is archive dust

a ruin
    part chemical
        part hay

What's stolen
    from machine sheds
        or field itself

    anhydrous ammonia
            legerdemain
                    into meth

xylazine
      an anesthesia for goat
            dog or stallion into tranq

Danville Community
      Center a sheriff
            tells us of

a house
      8 bodies
            lifeless

seems genuinely
      shaken we didn't
            sign up for this

she said
      even her shoes
            look like weapons

each body revived
      with Narcan
            they were polite

when they woke
      laughed nervously
            all of them

went home
        we signed up
                to chase kittens

from woods
        not mouths
                lined with limp balloons

filled with
        crystals
                as Roethke said

money
        money
                money

water
        water
                water

Catfish will eat
        rubber or wire
                ash

or coins
        endless capacity
                for aftermath

Women fill church
        fan away
                pollened air

    pageant of
           gold
                    feathered hair

take notes
        on sons
                behind stones
who come back
        in time for spring
                They built stairs

right down into
        river for
                baptism or fish

they step
        angler or folk
                down into

north fork
        edged by white
                quiet barns

unused now but for
        fox warren
                air wild

with distemper
        don't stay long
                a ruin

   some call it
        or else
              archive

it is still 1920 in here
        time for women
              to wash sheep

lead them from
        barn to river
              carry each ram

into water
        dip him until
              wool becomes so heavy

he can't stand
        under his own weight
              back on bank

staggers him
        as if thrown
              or newborn

until women press
        hands on fleece
              of prostrate animal

wring oiled
        water fist by
              fist ram

   struggling to stand
       it takes all women
            to hold him down

work river from wool
       until he can flee
            back to grass

they clean
       until exhausted
            lay in warm weeds

let work pass
       between them
            a flood

over which
       they hang
            minds in air

III.

Field Guide for How to Pioneer the Midwest

Gun. Axe. Tent.

Salted pig. Barrel of corn meal. Seed corn. Bushel of seed potatoes.

Land at five shillings an acre. A day's pay.

If there are woods, make your house out of trees. Bank the potatoes among the stumps.

Cut a ring of bark from around surrounding trees. They will die within months. This is where your field will be.

*

If there is grass, make your house out of grass.

Let sod be cut and stacked
like bricks. Let wood
from the wagon that brought you
be cut for supports. Let grass
be your roof. If it rains
four days outside, it will rain eight in.
Let grass become privacy
against the heat and cold and make love
with the scent of grass in your hair.
Imagine you are living inside of a peacock.
Let the tiny field growing from the roof
go knock-kneed in the wind.

This is your particular endlessness.
You cannot see a single tree.

Let grass become a way of speaking,
the one prayer
you have always been saying
under everyday speech,
ecstatic inarticulate petition for more life,
all commas.

*

"Chore" and "enchantment"

I sawed plastering lath, & loaded a load of hay. & it was a pleasant day.

have the same root

I hauled a load of hay to town 3352 lbs & sold it for $16.70. & it was a rainy day.

if you ignore

I went with sister Elizabeth to Fairfield to the doctor. & it was a fine day.

the actual laws of language

I hauled a load of hay to town 2206 lbs & sold it for $11. & it was a very warm day.

and instead obey

I sawed white pine on the sawmill & it was a windy day.

your own personal understanding

I & Magdalena went to market & it was a very rainy day.

of what in this life

I hauled cooper stuff from brant. & it was warm day.

should be woven together

I harrowed corn ground. & it was a very windy day.

*

If there are no trees or grass, make your house out of earth,

clay, horse dung, mud, sand, lime.
Straw, or, if none, your own hair.
Weave twigs from trees within a day's ride
and spread across it a daub
made of body and earth. If you cannot
avail yourself of sun,
light a torch and touch it to
the walls—it will feel like you
are burning what you have just built—
to harden. Inside
of your walls are weevils,

a glacier's cortege of stones,
roots that could still thrust up
some pale weed into your kitchen.
Come winter, the dark energy
of a house lit inside by fire
draws towards it those who
are afraid. Survival is a rage
for light. Your walls will thin,
giving its inches back to the cold.
Your hands will ache.
Hold them up to flames.
It will feel like you are burning.

*

The old cow always wore the bell—

First we put turpentine, mixed with sufficient grease so as not to take the hair off—

Father said afterward, it was strange that the Indian should know where he lived—

But I followed them, through black-ash swales where the water was knee-deep—

I always carried a gun, sometimes father's rifle—

The cattle were feeding on cow-slips and leeks, which grew in abundance, also on little French bogs that had just started up—

We had hard work to make him understand what we meant—
The other ox had the bloody murrain—

I am now over fifty years old—

The report of a rifle close by us—

To think they were lost in the wilderness—

*

If your field fails,
you are a true farmer.
You begin to learn
you have to invent these acres.
You invent the dead rabbit,
gun and boiling water.
You map the disseminations
of grass. Your footprint
is a patent of the machine
of your walking. You came here
with curiosity and hope
and were given work.
Your living is the field
and the field is unworkable
unless you learn
the sweet abandon
of routine. Novice of dust,
take these rose hips,
this burdock and sorrel.
For a season you can be sustained

by what grows wild.

—black frost plenty: A Primer for Farmwives

He left and gone.

*

Wove some. Mr. A. ploughing and took the head ache very hard, cool and fair. Not well.

*

As soon as the children's feet hit the floor, scrub them with lye soap so they will smell of it all day and everyone will know how clean a family you keep.

*

I came home rode the horse. Very lonesome and in much trouble, want to hear from Father.

*

Send the children aged at least five years out to the train tracks to collect lumps of spilled coal dropped by the B&O to burn in the stove. Burning coal means you can sleep through the night with no fire tending.

*

I was very sick with sick stomache and misary though me.

*

Put a dab of turpentine on your tongue to ward off germs.

*

Worked some on papas plants, Hosea came down, planted some wine seed.

*

Keep your milk and butter in a wooden box with holes screwed into it underwater
in the creek to keep them from blinking.

*

Fair and hard the beautiful spring.

*

If he is not back by now, you will have to drag timber up from Leverett to Eastman's to sell for flour or sugar.

*

Lucy Ann Rackly, James Rackly, Hiram Page came, cool and cloudy. Not very well. John Thomas walking.

*

Feed the hogs the worst you have.

*

Ellick died on the 8 of Dec — 3 O'clock. A. M. Jan. 11, 12, 13,14, 15 & 16 clear & cold —

17 Cloudy rainy — 18 All powerful Snow Storm, wind high, desperate cold.

*

Milk the cows. Clean the udders with iodine. Rub bacon fat on your hands to reduce friction. Keep the bucket between your legs to stop the sow from kicking it over. Choose diagonal teats and work until deflated.

*

A had hard head ache all night. Some better, not much work of any kind.

*

The art of chopping wood is not in strength but in leverage. Let the weight of the axe do the work. Lift it high above your head and guide where it falls. Cleave with the straightest grain. Done right, you only need so much power.

*

Do not read much, and the time is so rapidly going.

*

If he is not yet home by now, send a note to John Thomas via your restless black haired boy to search the jails and threshing crews.

*

Prospect generally, is decidedly bad. But oh! The flower Garden.

*

At the end of the day, take the children down to the creek and wash the chiggers off of their bodies.

*

— *black frost plenty.*

*

He comes home.

*

Boil the lights very tender,

*

Cook no more than beans for him. You should have known he would come. Real disasters are not so predictable. Hear him out then go to your crewel. You are making a wilderness of vine and fern that has no foreseeable end.

*

lard it all over with narrow slips of middling,

*

There is water to pump, his shirts to rake across the flat rock. You try to read the stains to tell where he's really been. Don't bother. You are no oracle of lost days. The red could be a crushed mosquito, a puff of rouge. It doesn't matter. Your one job is to clean everything. And everything is made primarily of dust.

*

and set the heart upright in the middle of the dish.

The End of the Midwest

For three days in the early 1800s, the Midwest ceased to exist. The strongest earthquakes on record tore open the Reelfoot Rift near New Madrid, Missouri. The Mississippi River ran backwards for several hours. A lake in Michigan began to boil and immediately a vast number of large tortoises rose to the surface and swam rapidly to the shore, where they were taken for food by the locals.

*

I know thy works, that thou hast a name that thou livest, and art dead.

*

December 16th, 1811:

The roar I thught would leave us deaf if we lived.
It was not a storm.
When you could hear, all you cold hear was screams from people and animals.
It was the worst thing that I have ever wittnesed.
It was still dark and you could not see nothng.
You could not hold onto nothing neither man or woman was strong enough –
the shaking would knock you lose like knocking hicror nuts out of a tree.
We was all banged up and some of us knocked out for awile and blood was everywhere.
We still had our home it was some damage.

Some people that the home was not built to strong did not.
We will have to hunt our animals.
If this earth quake or what ever it was did not happen in the Territory of Indiana then me and my family is moving to Pigeon Roost.

*

Be watchful, and strengthen the things which remain, that are ready to die: for I have not found thy works perfect before God.

*

Every church bell rang from St. Louis to Philadelphia. Dolley Madison, the first lady, was awoken by the tremor in the White House. Clocks stopped in Chicago. Chimneys slid from roofs in Cleveland. In Pittsburgh underground lights shone up from the chasms as deposits of quartz squeezed and sparked. The sun did not shine on America east of Nebraska for four days.

*

and the sun became black as sackcloth of hair

*

January 23rd 1812:

What are we gonna do?
You cannot fight it cause you do not know how.
It is not something that you can see.
In a storm you can see the sky and it shows dark clouds and you know

that you might get strong winds but this you can not see anything
but a house that just lays in a pile on the ground – not scattered around
and trees that just falls over with the roots still on it.
The earth quake or what ever it is come again today.
It was as bad or worse than the one in December.
We lost our Amandy Jane in this one – a log fell on her.
We will bury her upon the hill under a clump of trees
where Bessy Ma and Pa is buried.
A lot of people thinks that the devil has come here.
Some thinks that this is the beginning of the world coming to a end.

*

I will spue thee out of my mouth.

*

The earthquake created the world's largest sand boil, as a slurry of pressurized water and sand erupted volcanically, foundering the overlying sediment. Today, in
the midst of farmland, 136 acres of sand remains in the Missouri
Bootheel, about eight miles west of Hayti. Locals call it "The Beach."

*

For the great day of his wrath is come; and who shall be able to stand?

*

Febuary 8th, 1812:

If we do not get away from here the ground is going to eat us alive.
We had another one of them earth quakes yesterdy.
We are all about to go crazy – from pain and fright.
We can not do anything until we can find our animals or get some more.
We have not found enough to pull the wagons.

*

And the four beasts said, Amen.

*

The land undulated; chasms opened and swallowed horses and cows whole. Some fissures were as long as five miles. People discovered that most of the crevices opening ran from north to south, and when the earth began moving, they would quickly chop down trees in an east-west direction and hold on using the tree as a bridge. There were missing people who most likely fell untold stories underground.

*

If therefore thou shalt not watch, I will come on thee as a thief

*

March 20th, 1812:

I do not know if our minds have got bad or what.
But everybody says it.

Boyne River Daybook

1.

What brought me to the river
Is as clear as river itself,
Not pain alone, nor this brown trout

The size of a dollar bill stunned from my hook
Just pulled
        from its bottom jaw,
But the aftermath of pain, the holding pattern the fish weaves

At my feet as if it doesn't want to move too far
                                      from hurt's source,
As if comfort can only be found one step away from
The shadow that lifted you out of your life.

2.

A bird's bones like fork tines on the shore—
                                          I cast into
A seam of foam.
The heat makes of me a solitary object on a white plate.

On the surface of the Boyne a stonefly nymph
                                            struggles out of its molt,
Nothing rising up beneath it.
My father's death skitters
                            like a black mink on the far bank
But I do not move.
The river is blown out, glut-brown, uncrossable.
I stay for the sake of trying.

3.

Bats cruise rip-rap,
Clean mosquitoes off top water. I am thigh deep in
Water the color of hoof polish.
       I trusted Emerson, Weil.

I trusted my headlamp,
Its column of tea-rinsed light. I believed undivided
Attention was prayer.

It didn't work.
      I've stared and stared at these waters
And nothing is hidden. The double negative of
The faithless: nothing, search as I have, not here.

4.

Alcohol as mountain, cragged as the tip of a cigar, storm-scarfed—
That tall.
       Its shadow a county
I hide in, easier to go through than around. Alcohol as

Valley a river can't help but cut in two. I am its scavenger
That hunts blue crayfish, my wet teeth
Breaking chitin into bright splinters. I have a season-

to-season mind. I survive on grit, leavings, different fires.
Alcohol as zodiac,
Astral thickets stars tangle on, impenetrable
                                    as if they could be shelter.

5.

There are times when this river is as bare
as a motel room. Li Po made it seem glamorous: *though we
cut it with swords and sorrow returns,*
                              though we drown it with
wine,

*since the world can in no way answer to our craving, I will
loosen my hair tomorrow and take to a fishing boat—*
In reality, the trees smell like semen
                              and I crave what the dead crave:

Nothing. And so receive. I will be full one day—
The hours will be pageant. I'll fit my life
Like a blue egg in the palm.

6.

Where the Boyne pours into Lake Charlevoix,
                              old men fish.
Cloth chairs, radios, tiny coolers.
Down the shore, ice cream parlors, cafés,

Teen boys on their stomachs to net baitfish from a culvert.
Smelt, alewife, shad. Their game
                         is to catch the smallest.
A boy falls in and they howl. The old men think

Heaven is a stupid idea. How much weird smoke
Are we supposed to believe in? Look at these boys.
                         They're never going to die.
They would never swallow one bit of Christ.

7.

Now that I am old
                I have a new relationship
With weeping. I weep for infomercials and white butterflies.
Lonesome roads gray as heaven.

The tax system. My ghost in flames under the ash tree.
I weep for the joy of weeping.
For the marathon runner,
                            trucker, farmer, angler—

All who are professionally acquainted with endlessness.
When I was young, I wept for pain. Now I weep for beauty
And his bastard son darkness
                            and his wife my life.

8.

My father hated hunters—the only time I heard him say
The word *fuck* was over his brother
And his car dealer fighting
                      over deer rights to our woods.

He once snapped my plastic machine gun
Across his knee. His only blood sport was walleye
Out of Gunflint Lake. When he died I convinced myself

It was some kind of test—childhood was now killed enough
To be a man. Others said God had need of him.
If so, what the fuck of us, for whom God's hunt has not yet come?

9.

The steelhead can smell me,
                         sunscreen & diesel.
To get close I move at
A moon's pace, knees in rocked mud. Days when

My father's absence is most
                         vehement I pretend as if it
Can't see me. The steelhead
Stare upstream and turn into riverbed,

So camouflaged it is easier
                         to see shadow than fish itself.
You can hide, but not
From what you cause to lack light.

10.

My doctor's words echo: *toxic to*
                              the liver, toxic
To the heart. I cannot help
Holding a trout longer than I should to study its spots,

Black and orange, a wild Braille,
My bone marrow runs thin, white cell, red cell.
I loose the fish back to

Its hard embassy. My examination exhausted it.
It doesn't matter, it's safe.
After being tested by
                    one too large to see, it's safe.

11.

The pike is so deep I can't reach him. So I tie a spoon
To a thin rope and lower it
                         to tempt him with a small flash
Dragged through his black address. The pike is the lake's square root,

Gnats its remainder. A seagull with gravel in its guts
Oversees. The leeches are Gordian knots.
Sky a sunburn bathed in vinegar.

I want to see the killer's medieval teeth.
                                       Pike are coyotes.
Not hungry, but hunt. Not hiding but low,
Belly the white of extinction, hard squalls, end papers...

12.

Nothing panics like an ant in water—
It twitches
      like the death of a star,
Like a spark feasting on air—

All this even though
It can swim for a week straight and survive.
                      I too have lived this way,
Made scenes about how posthumous I am,

Flail and bloodwork. Terrestrial, terrestrial—
Cry wolf,
      weep wolf, speak no half-wolf: mean it.

13.

I could not find the river. I smacked
                              at ironweed, poison ivy,
Found a green-haired pond, a burnt duplex
Whose roof was so open to the sky that fog

Had found its way inside what used to be the living room:
Dreaming couch, last television on earth—but the river
Stayed locked in its wood box.
                    My lazy compass painted its one fingernail.

That night I pulled a fattened deer tick from my side
And watched it frantically search
The bathroom counter for its mask of blood.

14.

Alcohol as a Sunday,
                    the loneliest day, therefore God's own
As He clears leaves from
The old garden. His chores are as sober as yesterday's

Weather. Alcohol as a shoebox
Of bucktail preserved in borax and salt,
Kept up where the mice can't get it.

Alcohol as ferryman of the livid fen,
Who round about his eyes had wheels of flame. Alcohol
As Elizabeth Bishop's "The Fish": "He didn't fight. / He hadn't
                                                  fought at all..."

15.

When I can't sleep, it helps me to know that two hours
Away, in a museum, is Maybelle Carter's guitar.
And that up in Michigan trout rut muck across

River bottom. And that this river becomes a lake which becomes
Another river which becomes the great lake my only brother lives on.
It helps, but most times I take the stairs down to the kitchen

And drink red wine until I feel ready to be nothing for a while.
Technically though, I'm not nothing.
I'm there, just less. More than shadow,
                                                      but not light.

16.

I stand under a spider's protein chandelier,
Mend my leader tipped with a gnarl of animal hair. I catch fry,
fingerlings—
Some die. The vulnerable
                  get killed is one of the facts

Underpinning all life, it seems. That I am one of them, another.
It's important to me to outlive my father,
                                      for my children
To have more father than I did. My memory of him is the part

Of my mind most like a corn harvest
In that it is the slow destruction of form. I have a decade to go before
I surpass the size of his life,
                        a bag of dust we called field.

17.

Clouds the color of burned lamb bones.
                                              Clouds the color of straw
Left out in the rain. The sunrise a junkie cotton.
Today my grief is dilated as owl sight. Other times it is moss.

A crayfish's pincer floats by. My hangover lifts its snakehead.
My eyelids are former pearls. The dam shunts volts
                                        to the resort. My hangover
Yawns like a donkey. A cardinal drinks river oil.

My eyes are wadded up receipts. My joy is in a warren.
It is a wild rodent, like my grief. Side by side, they graze watercress.
My hangover is a dock gar. Dawn, old vacant lot streetlamp,
                                                              attempts light.

18.

My father watered his plants even while it was raining.
He loved flowers the way I do rivers, mail-ordered
Bougainvillea, hothouse roses, brugmansia
                              to East Central Illinois,

Converted our garage to a greenhouse. Late in his life
He told me he didn't believe in hell, only heaven
And started smoking cigarettes. He said he would understand

If, when the farm was mine, I sold it. I haven't.
His grave is silver grass,
His right hand soil, his left hand rain,
                              clenching, unclenching.

19.

The bagworms set up their crystal tenements.
A noon moon.
                      I have not had a drink yet.
My thumb's pike scars aren't healed.

A fox like a small rip in the fabric
Between hell and here. There is more to life than just life.
This is where all the pain comes from.
                                      You can take pain and lay it out

Like blank pages on a table.
                        From above it looks like windows
Of a building full of snow.
I shovel. You do too. We're all in here digging.

20.

Needle nose gar: I understand your need.
You'd devour me whole. There is no reason to spare
Whatever fits in your jaw: shad, herring, your own young.

You stick to shallows,
Test weed and rock-cluster, worst water,
Clay and oil. I too know how to disappear.

My ugliness has also been lifted up and sung of.
I too have been measured by a scale made of
The twenty seven diminutive bones in the human hand.

21.

I practice knots on the porch, nail, surgeon, double blood,
Bimini twist, haywire—braid to braid, mono
To mono. It's hot and the fishing
                              is bad. Days I've not yet lived

Wait wet in a nest, mouths to the sky,
Famished to exist, careless of what they hold for me.
There is so little I control it feels good to do

A simple task well. As the romance between death's fawn
And the endless field of my childhood
Unfolds elsewhere
                    I sit on the porch and do what I know.

22.

Alcohol as dogfish,
        eater of whole rivers, cliffs, basalt trees—
Alcohol as fossil hunger, dogfish
As death generalist,

Alcohol as monster for having nostrils,
As smoke program, dogfish as *yes*
I hate dark, alcohol as *no I love light,*
                              dogfish without hope,

Alcohol as the stream I go a-fishing in,
        dogfish as the first letter of the alphabet,
Alcohol as I have always regretted I was not as wise,
Dogfish as the day I was born.

23.

Every trout in Michigan has vanished. I haven't
Been here in two months. Back in
Ohio, I stripped the house of my body

For copper wire. It has taken me two weeks
To catch a single brown. I held the fish by the mouth above
The water and took a picture. I do this to prove

What I wanted to happen happened.
            It is cruel. I shouldn't have to
Use others to prove I was here.
Like daylight, my vanishing should be enough.

24.

It's all fatal, the early summer buttermilk light,
V on V of crow, fatal,
                      the sun that grunts forward like a lineman,
Waves knuckling North. The stones.

My daughters' white nightgowns. Flooded timber,
Its piles of yellowed foam. Even survival
Is fatal, thank goodness. Every inch, every shimmer.

Otherwise, it's just the so what prairie.
A little blood and air.
Shelter here, mineral there, meaningless mercy.

25.

The future has no eyes or tongue or hair. Like a trout,
It wants most to cease being
                          examined. In every future
You see much beauty and die. By now the trout is thrashing.

Its eyes seem dead already
Which is how the future's eyes would look if it had them.
Why keep asking when the answer

Is always the same? In all your life you had a few hours free
So you walked alone. You approached
Wild animals. You saw the moment they chose to flee.

Notes

The book's epigraph is from William Stafford's poem "One Home" from *The Way It Is: New and Selected Poems* (Graywolf Press).

"For the Silo Boys": Written in response to the *New York Times* article "Silos Loom as Death Traps on American Farms" by John M. Broder, October 28, 2012.

"Field Guide for How to Pioneer the Midwest": This poem features language from *The Bark Covered House* by William Nowlin, 1876.

"–black frost plenty: A Primer for Farmwives": This poem features language from the Diary 1834-1893 of Penelope Eliza Howard Alderman and the Diary 1851-1859 of James Evans, both from the Southern Historical Collection, University of North Carolina at Chapel Hill.

"The End of the Midwest": This poem features language from the journal 1811-1812 of George Heinrich Crist and can be found on the website of Jackson County, Missouri jacksongov.org.

"Boyne River Daybook" section 5 features language from "A Farewell To Secretary Shuyun At The Xietiao Villa In Xuanzhou" by Li Po, trans. Robert Kotewall and Norman L. Smith.

Acknowledgments

I am grateful to the editors of the following journals where these poems first appeared, sometimes in earlier versions.

Antioch Review: "A Brief History of the Midwest"

Belt: "Hell is Real," "Boyne River Daybook #19, 23, 24, 25"

Conjunctions: "The End of the Midwest," "—black frost plenty: A Primer for Farmwives"

The Cortland Review: "What I Know"

Kenyon Review: "Field Guide for How to Pioneer the Midwest"

Mississippi Review: "Do You Consider Writing to Be Therapeutic?"

The New Criterion: "Boyne River Daybook #7"

New England Review: "The Hive"

The New Yorker: "Not a Mile," "For the Silo Boys"

The Offing: "Boyne River Daybook #4"

storySouth: "Boyne River Daybook #20"

TriQuarterly: "Boyne River Daybook #15, 21"

"Do You Consider Writing to Be Therapeutic?" also appeared on *Poetry Daily* (poems.com).

I would like to thank the PhD program in creative writing at the University of Cincinnati and the Ohio Arts Council for their support.

Thanks to my colleagues in the English Department at Kenyon College and the *Kenyon Review* team.

Thanks to my students and the Kenyon Review Young Writers program.

Thanks to Linda Osier and Tommy's Advocates for Silo Safety.

Thanks to Diane Goettel and the entire staff at Black Lawrence for believing in this book.

Thanks to Michael McGriff, Adam Clay, Marcus Jackson, Noah Falck, Richie Hofmann, Liz Forman, Tyler Meier, David Lynn, Brian Michael Murphy, Jamie Lyn Smith-Fletcher, Sandeep Sodhi, and Aaron Rosa for their encouragement and friendship.

Thanks to Hanif Abdurraqib, Natalie Shapero and Chris Dombrowski for their generous words about this book and overall support of my work.

Thanks to Paul and Lesley Weber, the Weber-Stovers, Randy Rominger and Sarah Perkins.

In memory of Lyle and Betty Grace, Genevieve Shade and Roger Grace.

In memory of Gary Grace, my good man forever.

All my love for Susan Grace Rominger and Tim Grace.

All my love for Tory, Lily and Claire.

ANDREW GRACE is the author of *A Belonging Field* (Salt Publishing), *Shadeland* (Ohio State University Press) and *Sancta* (Ahsahta/Foundlings). His work has appeared in the *New Yorker*, *Poetry*, the *Adroit Journal*, *Boston Review* and *New Criterion*. A former Stegner Fellow at Stanford, he is a Senior Editor at the Kenyon Review and teaches at Kenyon College.